WOMEN WHO WAR

Women Warring for Their Marriage

Adrienne S. Young

Copyright

WOMEN WHO WAR. Copyright © 2019 by Adrienne S. Young.

Published by
Adrienne Young Ministries
info@adrienneyoungministries.org

Printed in the United States of America

Cover Design: Rickie D. Sarratt, Casting Crowns Media, LLC
Interior Design: B.O.Y. Enterprises, Inc.

ISBN: 978-1-7338264-0-2

Scripture

All scripture is taken from the New Living Translation and New Revised Standard Version.

DEDICATION

To the woman who put me and other women in a
portable and taught us how to pray, how to intercede,
how to recognize the enemy, and how to war... I will be
forever grateful for the Warrior in you. My Spiritual
Mother - Minister Elizabeth Seawright aka Ma
Seawright.

THANK YOU

I wrote this book during seminary, sitting on my couch while my boys were watching TV saying "Look, Mom! Watch this!" Thank you to my amazing family for allowing me pockets of time to write and eating pizza for dinner on Fridays so that I can complete this book. Eddie, thank you for allowing me to share our story. I know it hasn't always been easy being married to me, and I thank you for loving me in the good and the bad.

Thank you to my modern-day Women Who War who contributed to this book: Deronda, Twinette, and Victoria. Your stories will set thousands of women free. I know what you went through was painful at the moment, but the purpose it birthed outweighs the pain. I love you all.

Thank you to my brother, Rickie D. Sarratt of Casting Crowns Media, LLC, for once again creating a powerful book cover and capturing more than I could ever verbalize.

Otescia Johnson, you by far are the baddest woman I know! Not only because you are a superb business woman, but you taught me how to get where I am, and I did it on my face.

Lastly, thank you to the One who taught me how to war. I love you so much Lord. Had it not been for you, I would have died on the battlefield a long time ago. Thank you for giving me the opportunity to pen your words. I look forward to partnering with you for future books and projects you want to release through me. Thank you for creating me to be a Woman Who Wars.

HOW TO GET THE MOST OUT OF THIS BOOK:

I believe in having tools in my arsenal to use against the enemy, and this book is now part of our arsenal. Use a highlighter, write in the margins, circle everything you want to remember as a strategy in warfare against the enemy. My prayer is that you refer to this book so much that the cover easily bends and pages are curled back to where you will have to press them to close the book.

Before we dive all the way in, let's look into the difference between warring and fighting:

FIGHTING	WARRING
No plan and can be spontaneous.	Well thought out, planned out and the attacks are strategic.
A fighter reacts.	A warrior responds.
Between you and the other person	It is collaborative; it includes a general, captain, soldiers, armor bearers, artillery personnel.
Sometimes it is a selfish fight; looking only out for number one.	It is for more than just you, but for those connected to you and in your assigned territory and warriors cover one another.
You try anything and hope it works.	You know what works and what doesn't work.

Weapons are mostly hands, knife, stick, gun, bottle, shoe, whatever you can get your hand on at that moment.	Weapons depend on the type of war you are in and from what distance you need to make contact: hand grenades, guns, bombs, fighter jets, bow & arrow, swords, missiles.
A crowd may gather to witness it, but most stay out of it because "that has nothing to do with me;" they will only get involved if they need to protect him or herself.	People join in with you, and you train together; you strategize together, and you go in knowing someone has your back.
Is for bragging rights or defending oneself, but there is not always a clear winner.	There is a clear solid winner because, in our war, we don't fight **for** victory; we fight **from** a position of victory.
May not last long.	May last for days, weeks, month and years; therefore, warriors know how to endure.

No preparation - just take off swinging and hope for the best.	Warriors prepare; they recognize the difficulty, yet they take solace in knowing God is in the fight with them.
You may have never met the person before that moment. All you know is this person has threatened you and your space, and you don't care who he or she is.	A warrior studies her enemy. She knows where her enemy has been, and where he is going. She knows his ways and is one step ahead of him.
A fighter tires out easily, and the fight doesn't last long.	A warrior endures for LONG battles and takes breaks to rest up for the next assignment. They've trained so they know when to stop and when to proceed.
A fighter is all over the place and moves wherever the action is.	A warrior is strategic, takes calculated steps and has an assigned territory.

A fighter in the moment listens to no one.	A warrior is discerning, sensitive to hearing things, aroused, and alert and will consult with other warriors to get intel and/or direction.
Look out only for themselves	Will pause warring to check on a wounded warrior and take that wounded warriors with them and fight with them on their back while declaring "I'm not leaving without you!"

I am a recovering fighter. My husband and I would argue, and he would say, "Baby, we need to pray," and I didn't want to pray. I didn't want to war. I wanted to fight! In fighting, other people will hear you, see you, but will not help you. But if you ask someone to pray with you, you're inviting a warrior to war with you.

The title of this series is Women Who War, not Women Who Fight. Many of us say "I'm tired of fighting," and it's because God did not train us to fight, He trains us to war! That's why it's called WARfare and not FIGHTfare.

As of today, I am commissioning you to awaken the warrior, not the fighter, within. I speak to the warrior in you and say ARISE!

Arise in Hebrew means to "come on the scene, to emerge, to get up or stand up, and to become powerful." I speak to your warrior within, and I say "Come on the scene, emerge, get up, stand, become powerful, because greater is He that is in you than He that is the world." We are Women Who War!

PREFACE

- Storm
- Rogue
- Captain Marvel
- Wonder Woman
- Shuri
- Okoye
- Nakia.

These women were Warriors in their day and paved the way for many to come after them. They fought many battles, they won some and lost some, but the ones that counted made the greatest impact.

But, before these women warriors were others without a cape, without superpowers, and without fancy weapons. Their weapons were not carnal but mighty through God to the pulling down of strongholds. Weapons such as prayer, fasting, and faith, power, and authority from their Leader, caused them to save and birth nations, and they blazed the trail for us.

Jael.

Sarah.

Abigail.

Hannah.

Zipporah.

These Women Who War are the true sheros for us as their war stories have been told for thousands of years and will for eternity. We still study their strategies, dissect their lives and glean from their mistakes to learn how to war and win. We will also encounter modern-day women who war who share their stories of triumph over fertility, infidelity, betrayal, mother-in-law relationship issues, and more.

Join me and these women as we walk through their war zones to see how they triumphed over the enemy in their marriages and gave God glory along the way. We are Wives Who War!

CHAPTER 1
WARRING FOR DESTINY

WARRIOR: ADRIENNE

WAR ZONE: Home in Greenville, SC

ENEMY/OPPOSITION: Lost a child, grief and anger

STRATEGIES & WEAPONS: Intercession, declaring Scripture, deliverance and counseling

---

When the cops arrived at my home, I knew then the enemy had launched an all-out attack on my marriage.

I was a fighter. I grew up watching wrestling with my brother, and we would wrestle with our male cousin often. The two times I heard my parents fight, my mom would leave the house; therefore, I thought to fight and to leave was the proper responses to disagreements.

I fought my brother over a pen in elementary school.

I fought my younger male cousin who choked me over a game.

In college, I got mad at the guy I was dating and fought all 250 pounds of his 6-foot two frame.

When I was a working professional, I was dating another guy, and I fought him too. Needless to say, we broke up after that. Imagine the embarrassment I felt when his mom called me to get my side of the story, and I had to say, "Your son was right. I beat him up."

When I dated my husband, we didn't fight. I took the flight mode instead because we had a long distance relationship and wasn't around each other much. Six months into our marriage, I woke up on a Saturday morning, got out of bed, and blacked out. When I came to, I called my Mom and a friend who was a nurse to tell them what happened, and they encouraged me to go to urgent care. Eddie and I went, found out we were pregnant, but the baby was not showing up on the ultrasound. The doctor sent me to the hospital to see what was going on. I had mixed emotions as I called my parents and brother saying, "I'm pregnant, but they can't find the baby."

The ultrasound showed I had an ectopic pregnancy - I was pregnant, but the baby was in my tubes. The doctor rushed to do surgery as he didn't want the tube to rupture, but it was too late. It was an outpatient procedure, and when I arrived home that night, I felt my husband rubbing my head and saying over and over again, "I could have lost you... I could have lost you." My tube had ruptured, and I lost so much blood there was no way I should have lived - those are the exact words my doctor told me the following morning. In addition to the tubal pregnancy and loss of blood, I had a cyst the size of a grapefruit on my ovary. The doctor removed my tube and my ovary on opposite sides which lessened my chances of getting pregnant again. Depression overtook me. I was angry at God. I wanted a baby and now I didn't know if I would ever be a mother. This news took a toll on our 6-month-old marriage, and one day it blew up.

Has there been a time in your marriage when things blew up? I'm talking an all-out screaming, yelling and kicking blow up? When you look back on it, you wonder where did it start? What made us so mad? For me, I got mad at Eddie over vacuuming. Yep, you read it right. Vacuuming. Because of the surgery, I could not do household chores. I asked him to vacuum, but he was taking too long for me, and I went off. In the middle of the heated moment, Eddie said: "Baby, let's pray." I told him I didn't want to pray. A few minutes later, the phone rang, and it was my pastor calling to check on me. My husband answered, "Now is not a good time to talk," he said, "I'll call you back." God gave us two ways of escape, and we walked right past them unto the battlefield. After that, it was all a blur after.

I started swinging.

He grabbed my arms to stop me.

I bit him.

He shoved my face to stop me.

The fight was so loud that people who were walking by heard me screaming, and they called the police.

How did we get here?

Have you ever asked yourself that same question? When you "come to yourself" and see how that side of you manifested, the side you hate and thought was dead, do you ever wonder "How did I get here?"

The enemy has no new tricks. He doesn't play fair. He got me when I was at my lowest. He played on my emotions, and it appeared he won. I'm sure he has did the same to you. Should you find yourself in a heated fellowship, my prayer for you is to take the way of escape that God provides. Cry out to Him for help, and if He sends the police to your home, thank Him because it could save your marriage.

The police, Eddie's boss, and my mom arrived at our home. They asked us questions, and if it wasn't for God's grace and mercy and Eddie's boss vouching for us, they would have arrested us. The police made us stay apart that night, and we had a meeting in Eddie's boss's office the next day. To say it embarrassed me and made me ashamed is an understatement. My actions caused a huge rift in our marriage, but God never left us. I wish I could say that was our first and

4

only fight, but it wasn't. The enemy came again after our second son was born, and I was literally throwing punches while holding my baby in my arms. Thank God my Mother was there to stop it.

Despite those crazy moments, it never hindered the call on me and my husband's life. After I joined the intercessory prayer team at my church, I realized I was dealing with multiple enemies, and I warred. I researched every demonic force attached to anger and fighting, and I did my own deliverance session.

I fasted.

I prayed.

I read and confessed the word.

I did a clean sweep of our home.

My husband and I went through counseling.

I confessed my sins to him and asked for forgiveness.

When we moved from that home to another home, the fighting stopped. When we moved from there to Charlotte, the demon tried to rear its ugly head again, but I declared its eviction, and it left.

It's one thing to experience deliverance and another thing to maintain the deliverance. My sister, I don't know what you are facing in your marriage, but I do know that whatever it is, God will help you war, and you will be victorious!

Here's the list of strategies that helped me the most:

- *Prayer of intercession.* If you don't know how to pray, pray in your prayer language and from a marriage prayer book.

- *Find the root cause*, the demonic force you're dealing with, and ask God for a battle plan to uproot it.

- *Surround yourself with women warriors* who will get on the battlefield with you and pray with and for you, your spouse, and your marriage.

- *Grieve.* Take time to grieve. We lost a child, and we thought we could move on since there was no attachment to the baby. We were wrong.

- *If you are in the middle of a heated discussion, stop and pray.* Even if the spouse is not feeling it. Just open your mouth and begin to pray and declare.

6

- *Spend time together* and just talk about your feelings, especially if you faced a tragedy.

- *Admit you're wrong and walk in forgiveness.* Pride has no place in marriage.

Some of you admire my marriage and follow us on FourEver Young TV and didn't know our story. The half still hasn't been told, but I can truly say ALL things work together for them that love God and are called according to His purpose. God destined us to be together. He destined for me to share my story with you and to declare that I am a woman who wars, and I win.

Because the enemy robbed my husband and me of our first five years of marriage, I put "newlywed life" and other images of love on my vision board and have been daily declaring *I am madly in love with my husband, and he is madly in love with me!*

The Bible is my go-to for declarations. I hope some of these will bless you and will manifest in your marriage:

7

DECLARATIONS

- My husband and I are subject to one another out of reverence for Christ. As a wife, I am subject (submissive and adapt myself) to my own husband as a service to the Lord. For my husband is the head of me as Christ is the Head of the church. Ephesians 5:21-23 AMPC

- As the church is subject to Christ, so I am also subject in everything to my husbands. Ephesians 5:24 AMPC

- My husband loves me as Christ loved the church and gave Himself up for her. Ephesians 5:25

- My husband loves me as he does his body. He loves me as he loves himself. For no man ever hated his own flesh, but nourishes *and* carefully protects and cherishes it, as Christ does the church; therefore, my husband nourishes, carefully protects, and cherishes me as Christ does the church. Ephesians 5:28-29 AMPC

- My husband has left his father and his mother and is joined to me, his wife, and the two of us have become one flesh. Ephesians 5:31 AMPC

- My husband, without exception, loves me, his wife, as being in a sense his very own self; and I see that I respect *and* reverences my husband, that I notice him, regard him, honor him, prefer him, venerate, and esteem him; and that I defer to him, praise him, and love and admire him exceedingly.

- Genesis 1:27-28 says "So God created man in his own image, in the image of God he created him; male and female he created them. And God blessed them. And God said to them, 'Be fruitful and multiply and fill the earth and subdue it and have dominion over the fish of the sea and over the birds of the heavens and over every living thing that moves on the earth.'" Therefore, I declare God blesses my husband and me. We are fruitful, multiply and have dominion on the earth.

- One can put to flight 1,000 and 2 10,000; therefore, my husband and I put to flight 10,000 plus of anything that comes to attack our marriage - every demonic force has to flee in Jesus' name. Deuteronomy. 32:30

- In our marriage, we live with complete lowliness of mind (humility) and meekness (unselfishness, gentleness, mildness), with patience, bearing with one another *and* making allowances because we love one another. Ephesians 4:2 AMPC

- My husband and I are eager *and* strive earnestly to guard *and* keep the harmony *and oneness* of, and produced by, the Spirit in the binding power of peace. Ephesians 4:3 AMPC

- And whatever my husband and I do, no matter what it is, in word or deed, we do everything in the name of the Lord Jesus *and* in dependence upon Him, giving praise to God the Father through Him. Colossians 3:17

- I am subject to your husbands - subordinate - and I adapt myself to them, as is right *and* fitting *and* my proper duty in the Lord. Colossians 3:18

- My husband loves me, is affectionate and sympathetic with me, and is not harsh *or* bitter *or* resentful toward me. Colossians 3:19

- I declare, according to Ecclesiastes 4:9, that the two of us are better than one because we have a good, more satisfying return for our labor: If either of us falls down, one can help the other up. Also, when we lay down together, we will keep warm.

- Our love is patient and kind. It does not envy; it does not boast; it is not proud. It does not dishonor others; it is not self-seeking; it is not easily angered, it keeps no record of wrongs. If I have the gift of prophecy and can fathom all mysteries and all knowledge, and if I have a faith that can move mountains, but do not have love, I am nothing."

- I do everything in love. 1 Corinthians 16:14

- I live out 1 Peter 2:23 and 3:1-6: "When they hurled their insults at Jesus, he did not retaliate; when he suffered, he made no threats. Instead, he entrusted himself to him who judges justly. In the same way, I submit myself to my husband so that, if he does not believe the word, I may win him over not with my words but by my behavior - seeing the purity and reverence of my life. My outward beauty will not trump my inner self, the unfading beauty of a gentle and quiet spirit, which is of great worth in God's sight.

- In the same way, my husband lives considerately with me, with an intelligent recognition of our marriage relation, honoring me as physically the weaker, but realizing that we are joint heirs of the grace (God's unmerited favor) of life, in order that his prayers may not be hindered *and* cut off. Otherwise, he cannot pray effectively. 1 Peter 3:7 AMPC

- We are of one *and* the same mind (united in spirit), sympathizing with one another, loving each other as of one household, compassionate

11

and courteous (tenderhearted and humble). 1 Peter 3:8 AMPC

- Above all, we love each other deeply, because love covers over a multitude of sins. 1 Peter 4:8

CHAPTER TWO

CHOSEN TO WAR AND GUARANTEED TO WIN

WARRIOR: JAEL

WAR ZONE: Tent of Jael by way of Mount Tabor near Kedesh

ENEMY/OPPOSITION: Sisera - commander of King Jabin of Canaan's army

STRATEGIES & WEAPONS: Make the first move to invite the enemy in, be kind, and use what is in the house to take him out.

JAEL'S STORY:

I knew war broke out in my nation, but I didn't know it would end in my house. I never thought God would choose me, a housewife, to save a nation using everyday items lying around my tent. My sister, let me encourage you. With spiritual warfare, you may not have the "perfect" Scripture to quote or know the "perfect" prayer to pray. But, when God gets ready to use you, He will sometimes use what you have around you to take out the enemy in your home. Here's my war story.

JUDGES 4:4-10; 14-23

4 Deborah, the wife of Lappidoth, was a prophet who was judging Israel at that time. **5** She would sit under the Palm of Deborah, between Ramah and Bethel in the hill country of Ephraim, and the Israelites would go to her for judgment. **6** One day she sent for Barak son of Abinoam, who lived in Kedesh in the land of Naphtali. She said to him, "This is what the Lord, the God of Israel, commands you: Call out 10,000 warriors from the tribes of Naphtali and Zebulun at Mount Tabor. **7** And I will call out Sisera, commander of Jabin's army, along with his chariots and warriors, to the Kishon River. There I will give you victory over him."

8 Barak told her, "I will go, but only if you go with me."

9 "Very well," she replied, "I will go with you. But you will receive no honor in this venture, for the Lord's victory over Sisera *will be at the hands of a woman*." So Deborah went with Barak to Kedesh. **10** At Kedesh, Barak called together the tribes of Zebulun and Naphtali, and 10,000 warriors went up with him. Deborah also went with him.

14 Then Deborah said to Barak, "Get ready! This is the day the Lord will give you victory over Sisera, for the Lord is marching ahead of you." So Barak led his 10,000 warriors down the slopes of Mount Tabor into battle. **15** When Barak attacked, the Lord threw Sisera and all his chariots and warriors into a panic. Sisera leaped down from his chariot and escaped on foot. **16** Then Barak chased the chariots and the enemy army all the way to Harosheth-haggoyim, killing all of Sisera's warriors. Not a single one was left alive.

17 Meanwhile, Sisera ran to the tent of Jael, the wife of Heber the Kenite, because Heber's family was on friendly terms with King Jabin of Hazor. **18** Jael went out to meet Sisera and said to him, "Come into my tent, sir. Come in. Don't be afraid." So he went into her tent, and she covered him with a blanket.

19 "Please give me some water," he said. "I'm thirsty." So she gave him some milk from a leather bag and covered him again.

20 "Stand at the door of the tent," he told her. "If anybody comes and asks you if there is anyone here, say no."

21 But when Sisera fell asleep from exhaustion, Jael quietly crept up to him with a hammer and tent peg in her hand. Then she drove the tent peg through his temple and into the ground, and so he died.

22 When Barak came looking for Sisera, Jael went out to meet him. She said, "Come, and I will show you the man you are looking for." So he followed her into the tent and found Sisera lying there dead, with the tent peg through his temple.

23 So on that day, Israel saw God defeat Jabin, the Canaanite king. **24** And from that time on Israel became stronger and stronger against King Jabin until they finally destroyed him.

It was a guaranteed victory. Through Deborah, God told Barak when you go against the army and general Sisera, "I will give him into your hand," yet Barak would only go if Deborah went with him forfeiting the defeat from his hands into the hand of me, at that time, an unnamed woman.

Unbeknownst to me, I was assigned to take the enemy out, and you have been too. Everything you have been through up to this point in your life qualifies you for the assignment, and you are guaranteed the victory. Let me help you because I hear you say "I'm only a housewife. I don't have a college degree. I never finished school." You don't need a title, a position, or a license for this assignment. I wasn't a judge or a prophetess like Deborah. I wasn't in a leadership position. I wasn't an officer, a pastor, a teacher, or an apostle. I was a wife, a woman who knew God, who

16

worshipped him and when God chose me for this assignment, I unlocked the warrior within and took the enemy out!

Sisera fled on foot to my tent! The nerve of him. He persecuted the Israelites for 20 years, and I was affected by it as well, and my husband Heber had an alliance with him. Can you imagine being married to someone who allowed a nation to be persecuted and was in a position to do something about it and never did? It was like I was sleeping with the enemy. Yet, I never opened my mouth to voice my opinion on the matter. I heard the stories of how God rescued my people before, and I knew He would do it again. I'm honored he chose me to partner with Him.

I was not surprised that Sisera came to my tent, and that is why I came out to meet him. It was part of my strategy. I knew his ways from his interaction with him before, and I was a step ahead of him to stay on the offense. He was on my playing field now, in my territory; therefore, he had to play by my rules.

My sister, don't panic when the enemy shows up in your neighborhood and pulls into your driveway. Meet him at the door and invite him in! Why? Because you have been assigned to take him out. What type of warrior meets the enemy at her door and invites him in?

A worshipping warrior.

A confident in God warrior.

A prepared warrior.

A praying warrior.

A warrior who knows if the enemy is on my home turf, I have the advantage!

Your home has been saturated in prayer, saturated in praise, and saturated in worship. As a matter of fact, before the enemy shows up, you will probably be in a conversation with God in prayer, and he will warn you just like he did me. Go out to meet your Sisera!

I had a plan in place when he arrived. In addition to the spiritual weapons of prayer, praise, and discernment, I consulted with God for the weapons in the natural I would use. One of those weapons was kindness: *"Come into my tent, sir. Come in. Don't be afraid,"* I said. When I saw the fear in his eyes, I knew then God had him right where he wanted him. He ran to my home in fear; therefore, his defense mechanisms were down, and he was vulnerable. Continuing with kindness, I covered him with a blanket, and although he asked me for water, I gave him milk and yogurt in a bowl fit for nobles (Judges 5:25) and covered him again.

The enemy was exhausted and was so cozy in my house that he fell asleep. He should have never done that.

Do you know what I love about God in this situation? He exhausted the enemy for me. The Lord threw Sisera and all his chariots and warriors into a panic (4:15). I didn't have to work hard to take him out. I know Sisera was exhausted from the battle and running to escape, and I believe your enemy is exhausted too, but for different reasons.

He is thrown into panic and exhausted from your fervent praying.

He is thrown into panic and exhausted from your persistence in prayer.

He is thrown into panic and exhausted from you declaring the Word.

He is thrown into panic and exhausted from you being loving regardless of how you are treated.

He is thrown into panic and exhausted from you praising and worshipping when you have every right to throw down your sword and walk away.

Your situation didn't change, and you still warred.

Your depression didn't leave right away, and you still warred.

Your loved one died, and you still warred.

Cancer came back, and you still warred.

19

Like me, your Heber still allied with the enemy, but you stayed in the marriage. His ally was alcohol, porn, drugs, or infidelity, but you exhausted the enemy by not allowing these alliances to give up on him because you believe God to heal him and to save him. Take a minute right now and give God praise for exhausting your enemy.

After he fell asleep, I grabbed my weapons, a tent peg, and a hammer, and quietly crept up to him, and drove the tent peg into his temple into the ground, and he died. Now you may be thinking, "Why did you use a tent peg and hammer? Those are odd weapons." I used what I knew to use. I was used to pitching tents, and I knew exactly how to strike a tent peg once and make it go into the ground. What's lying around your home that you can use to take the enemy out?

The tent peg and hammer are the tools I chose, yet, it was HOW I took Sisera out that made the difference. I *quietly* crept up to take the enemy out. I strongly encourage you to do the same so that he won't even suspect you're coming. It's a sneak attack. How do you war quietly, you ask? You war quietly by partnering with God, the Lord who is the man of War (Exodus 15:3) and stands beside you like a great warrior (Jeremiah 20:11). Stay in constant communication with Him for every move and be His secret agent in the earth. No longer will you have to be brash or combative when you encounter the enemy. In quietness and in trust is your strength (Isaiah 20:15b).

Jeremiah 20:11 "But the Lord stands beside me like a great warrior. Before him, my persecutors will stumble. They cannot defeat me. They will fail and be thoroughly humiliated. Their dishonor will never be forgotten."

So Sisera died.

Not on a battlefield, but in my tent.

Not by a sword, but by a nail and a hammer.

Not loudly with the clinking of swords, but quietly under a blanket.

Not by the hands of a man, but by the hands of a woman...a woman who warred.

Declarations

- Because I am on the offense, I go out and meet the enemy.

- I am guaranteed the victory because God is on my side.

- I've been chosen to take the enemy out, and I am prepared.

- I play worship music in my home to saturate it for the enemy's arrival.

- God throws my enemy into a panic and exhausts him for me.

- My praying exhausts the enemy.

- My praise and worship exhaust the enemy.

- These declarations exhaust the enemy.

- I use what is in my home to take the enemy out.

- Kindness is my weapon of choice.

- I war quietly and kill with one blow.

Prayer

Father, thank you for giving me the strategy to defeat the Siseras that come to my tent - the place where I dwell. May I have the boldness of Jael to invite him in and cover him with my kindness. Thank you, God, that when the enemy arrives, he will arrive exhausted and in fear making him vulnerable and not ready for our sneak attack. Show me, God, what to use in my house, my tent peg and hammer, to defeat the enemy. Help me to quietly take him out and be bold like Jael to drive the peg through his temple to kill him. Allow my praise, my worship, and my declarations to be the shattering blow to my enemy as I declare "I am a Woman Who Wars" In Jesus name, Amen.

CHAPTER 3

From Wounded to Warring

WARRIOR: HANNAH

WAR ZONE: In Shiloh on the way to the Tabernacle

ENEMY/OPPOSITION FACED: Peninnah - wife of Elkanah and mother of his children; barrenness

STRATEGIES & WEAPONS: Tears, quietness, prayer and receiving a prophetic word.

Hannah's story

You would think by now I was used to it. Year after year it was the same - Peninnah would taunt me as we went to the Tabernacle. I would be reduced to tears, and Elkanah would try to comfort me with a choice portion of food, but it never worked. I would travel back and forth from the Tabernacle empty...empty in my womb and wounded in my soul. But this time, it was different. I decided to war beyond my wounds, and my womb opened.

Adrienne S. Young
1 Samuel 1:2-20 NLT

There was a man named Elkanah who lived in Ramah in the region of Zuph in the hill country of Ephraim. He was the son of Jeroham, son of Elihu, son of Tohu, son of Zuph, of Ephraim. 2 Elkanah had two wives, Hannah and Peninnah. Peninnah had children, but Hannah did not.

3 Each year Elkanah would travel to Shiloh to worship and sacrifice to the Lord of Heaven's Armies at the Tabernacle. The priests of the Lord at that time were the two sons of Eli—Hophni and Phinehas. 4 On the days Elkanah presented his sacrifice, he would give portions of the meat to Peninnah and each of her children. 5 And though he loved Hannah, he would give her only one choice portion[b] because the Lord had given her no children. 6 So Peninnah would taunt Hannah and make fun of her because the Lord had kept her from having children. 7 Year after year it was the same—Peninnah would taunt Hannah as they went to the Tabernacle.[c] Each time, Hannah would be reduced to tears and would not even eat.

8 "Why are you crying, Hannah?" Elkanah would ask. "Why aren't you eating? Why be downhearted just because you have no children? You have me—isn't that better than having ten sons?"

9 Once after a sacrificial meal at Shiloh, Hannah got up and went to pray. Eli the priest was sitting at his

25

customary place beside the entrance of the Tabernacle.[d] 10 Hannah was in deep anguish, crying bitterly as she prayed to the Lord. 11 And she made this vow: "O Lord of Heaven's Armies, if you will look upon my sorrow and answer my prayer and give me a son, then I will give him back to you. He will be yours for his entire lifetime, and as a sign that he has been dedicated to the Lord, his hair will never be cut."

12 As she was praying to the Lord, Eli watched her. 13 Seeing her lips moving but hearing no sound, he thought she had been drinking.14 "Must you come here drunk?" he demanded. "Throw away your wine!"

15 "Oh no, sir!" she replied. "I haven't been drinking wine or anything stronger. But I am very discouraged, and I was pouring out my heart to the Lord. 16 Don't think I am a wicked woman! For I have been praying out of great anguish and sorrow."

17 "In that case," Eli said, "go in peace! May the God of Israel grant the request you have asked of him."

18 "Oh, thank you, sir!" she exclaimed. Then she went back and began to eat again, and she was no longer sad.

19 The entire family got up early the next morning and went to worship the Lord once more. Then they returned home to Ramah. When Elkanah slept with Hannah, the Lord remembered her plea, 20 and in due time she gave birth to a son. She named him Samuel, for she said, "I asked the Lord for him."

I can't tell you how grateful I am to have a husband who loves me and God. Some women would be satisfied with that alone, but in my culture, it is shameful to be barren. As much as I love Elkanah and he loves me, it wasn't enough.Do you know how hard it is to be surrounded by, to see, smell, and hear the very thing you desire from God? To make it worse, my rival would taunt me. She was never bold enough to do it in front of Elkanah; therefore, he didn't understand my tears. But I knew Someone who did, and this time, I decided to go and pour out my heart to Him. I decided to walk wounded to the tabernacle and war through my tears in prayer. I'm glad I did because who God birthed through me, changed the trajectory of a nation.

Have you ever dreaded going somewhere? Everyone around you is excited, but you hate this time of year because it reminds you of what you don't have. Can you imagine going to an event knowing you will tormented from the time you leave until it was time to go home? I do all too well. After a sacrificial meal at Shiloh, I didn't have the strength to listen to the taunts anymore or answer Elkanah's questions knowing it would hurt his feelings. I wanted to scream, "NO! Having you is NOT better than having ten sons because should something happen to you, there will be no one to take care of me!"

Have you ever been asked a question that you know the person knows the answer to? It is frustrating. "Why are you crying?" "Don't you know that I love you?" Or, they will say something stupid like "Children are expensive these days, so it might be a good thing you don't have them." "If you know what I know, you would stay single as long as you can."

How do you handle words that wound? What do you do when those closest to you don't get it? You walk away. You walk past the person who wants to fix it to the One who can and will fix it.

I got up...let me stop here because that's profound in and of itself.

Year after year I sat and listened to the taunts of Peninnah. I sat in embarrassment and shame as my husband did not understand my pain. I sat with Peninnah's children and played with them. I sat and watched others eat while tears stained my face. I sat there and took it for YEARS! But this time, I got up.

What have you sat and faced year after year?

Where did you sit and allow the enemy to bully you with his words?

What did you sit and take with tears in your eyes and sorrow in your heart that left you empty?

I declare that this is the day you will get up!

Rise out of your comfortable state.

Stand above your situation.

Walk away from where you sat, and with every step, God will strengthen you like He did me.

This time my sister, when you get up, know that you when you sit down again, you will sit with authority over what had you. You see, changing positions in the midst of what feels like defeat signals to your brain, "I'm ready to shift." You are telling yourself "I know longer want to be comfortable in this state. I am ready to rise and walk away from this situation, this torment, this disappointment and go to God." My sister, arise to war and walk to a place of prayer!

I got up and went to pray, and Eli the priest was there sitting at his customary place beside the entrance of the Tabernacle. In deep anguish, I cried bitterly as I prayed in my heart to the Lord. My lips moved, but no sound came out of my mouth. This silent prayer was filled with visible emotions that I could not shush.

When warring, the sounds of our emotions can sometimes overtake us so much that our prayer may be a whisper of words. God hears our whisper warring prayer my sister. Although my actions caused Eli to think I was drunk, that was quickly disseminated once he heard the why behind my warfare prayer In kindness, I said to him " *I am very discouraged, and I was pouring out my heart to the Lord. I have been <u>speaking out of</u> my great anguish and sorrow all this time (1 Sam 1:16 NASB)."*

My honesty to him freed me, and it can do the same for you. I pray we no longer put a muzzle over our great anguish and sorrows, but that we will *speak out of* it. When I begin to speak out of my anguish, it brought me out of it. It was as if my silent words, my prayer to God, was my way of escape.

What do you need speak out of?

What is causing you anguish and sorrow?

Will you go to God in prayer to release it from your life?

I encourage you to go in prayer, remove the muzzle from what has kept you in bondage, and speak out of it until God causes what had you bound to break free through your words.

Know this my sister, God has someone, an Eli, stationed at the door of your place of prayer to give you confirmation that it is already done. Don't allow their mistaking you for being "drunk" deter you from receiving the Word they have for you. As soon as the words left my mouth, and as soon as Eli spoke "Go in peace! May the God of Israel grant the request you have asked of him," God responded, and I believe my womb was open at that very moment!

My sister, I believe God allows us to go through situations knowing it has an expiration date assigned to it and warring through prayer makes that expiration respond. I went back and began to eat again and was no longer sad. My countenance was lifted! I knew God had heard and answered my prayer. The following year, I was holding my answered prayer, my son Samuel in my arms. I am grateful to God that I decided to war through my wounds because it produced my promise. How much more will God do for you, my sister, my woman who wars?

Warring for an open womb. Reflecting on Hannah.

I wonder if Hannah would have died barren had she not prayed to bear a son. I shudder to think how many times we don't conceive because we are not praying it into existence. What do you need to pray to come from the spirit realm into the natural and birth? For Hannah, it was the prophet Samuel who would be the one to transition a kingdom from judges to a reign of kings. What made Hannah persevere past ridicule and years of taunting and pray, "God, this is the last year I will be in this state. The next time I come to this place, I will come with my promise." Will you, my sister, war for an open womb to conceive? Will you be willing to weep bitterly and be mistaken for a drunkard?

Perhaps God closes our spiritual wombs until we resolve in our heart that what we desire will belong to him. It will be for his glory. We would give whatever it is back to him.

Hannah did something that is key after Eli confirmed her prayer would be answered. *They rose early in the morning and worshiped before the Lord (1 Sam. 1:19a).* After you have warred for your open womb, your response to God is worship. I prophesy over you that today is the day you rise up from your barrenness, walk towards the temple, and pray to God specifically for what you desire knowing your conception, like Hannah's, will be an act of God. Dedicate the promise back to Him in advance and worship Him. As Eli said to Hannah, I say to you: "Go in peace. The God of Israel grant the petition you have made to Him."

In due time Hannah conceived and bore a son. She named him Samuel, for she said, "I have asked him of the Lord. 1 Samuel 1:20 NRSV

32

Declarations

- I get up from my situation, and it signals my brain that it's time to shift.

- I pray to God and allow my emotions to display.

- I remove the muzzle to hide my anguish, and I'm free to say how I truly feel.

- I am specific in my prayer request.

- God has positioned someone to confirm His answer to my prayer.

- I will eat again and no longer be sad.

- I go to worship the Lord knowing it's already done.

- This time next year, I will have what I asked God for in prayer and dedicate it back to God.

Prayer

Father, thank you for the example of Hannah that teaches me how to war silently and specifically in prayer as I pour out my heart to you. Thank you for positioning Elis in my life who will confirm the answer to my prayers. I will worship you in the time between my prayer and my answer. Thank you God that this time next year, I will hold the answer to my prayer and dedicate it back to you, in Jesus name, Amen.

CHAPTER 4

The Sound of Our Breakthrough and a Picture of Our Promise

WARRIOR: Deronda

WAR ZONE: Doctor's offices

ENEMY/OPPOSITION: My barren womb

STRATEGIES & WEAPONS: Faith, intercession, and never giving up

---

The sound of our breakthrough was so important because for over three years all we heard was the the deafening sound of words like infertility, IVF, IUI, and difficulty conceiving. It was three long years of disappointment.

I am PREGNANT! Je suis enceinte! We made feet for booties!! I'm not sure how many ways I could say the words I waited so long to be a part of my conversations. What felt even better was my husband and I were carrying our promise and no one had any idea! I wasn't sure how long we could keep this secret from family and friends especially with the

Thanksgiving Holiday approaching. But Geesh! It felt good! We shared glances and little laughs. We were also the only ones that knew why I slept most of the Thanksgiving Holiday. We are pregnant!

As we waited in the examining room, we giggled with anticipation and uncertainty. After a few

minutes Dr. Gleaton arrived and was her normal bright and bubbly self. She was just as happy and excited as we were. She wanted to hear the details of how we got to this point. She was and continues to be one of our cheerleaders and prayer warriors. Before we started the exam, there was a knock at the door and in walks Nurse Angie. She said she wasn't going to miss any part of the first exam.

Then it happened. The exam started. I looked at the monitor and saw the cutest little peanut shaped fetus nestled in my uterus. I saw the strongest heartbeat and instantly fell in love. I immediately shed tears of joy and thanked God for this moment. My husband was just as happy! A perfect moment—in an examining room with my husband and the amazing doctor and nurse who had been praying and believing it would happen.

The most important thing from this visit was a hearing the sound of our breakthrough, our baby's

heartbeat and seeing our promise, the picture of our baby. The first ultrasound pic still hangs on our prayer wall as an answered prayer.

The sound of our breakthrough was so important because for over three years all we heard was the deafening sound of words like infertility, IVF, IUI, and difficulty conceiving. The sound of cries

accompanied by fallen tears is what my husband Jarrett and I heard.

It was three long years of failed fertility treatments, unexplained infertility, attending baby showers of people who didn't plan nor desired to be pregnant.

It was three long years believing God had turned a deaf ear to all of my prayers desiring to fill my womb.

It was three years of battling depression all the while trying to be the people we needed to be for our congregation and family.

It was three long years of creating unique answers when people questioned why we didn't have children yet.

It was me falling apart and being put back together realizing that even though fertility specialist gave us only a 5% chance of ever conceiving that looking at the number 5 in the spiritual realm meant grace and His grace was sufficient even in this situation.

So I rejoice today. I rejoice knowing all the tears I cried was watering the seeds I had sown. I

37

rejoice that after completely allowing God to be God over every area of my life, he blessed my

womb to grow a healthy baby girl who knows the power and worth of prayer and praise. For it is

in those moments seeing her praising God that I know God was divinely weaving this masterpiece like only He can. I rejoice knowing my testimony is blessing the lives of so many women who like me once thought conceiving and giving birth would ever be possible.

CHAPTER 5

THE POWER OF INTERCESSION

WARRIOR: ABIGAIL

WAR ZONE: Carmel - where Nabal owned property

ENEMY PROFILE: King David by way of Nabal - the husband of Abigail. His name means "fool."

STRATEGIES & WEAPONS: Hospitality, intercession, and humbleness.

Abigail's story

His name says it all. Nabal was a fool. Why in the world did he have to be so rude to David's men when they protected our flocks, spoke blessings of peace and prosperity, and all they asked for were provisions we had more than enough of to spare? Unfortunately, taking the blame for my husband's foolish behavior was normal for me, and I shudder to think what would have happened had I not intervened this time. I'd heard the stories of King David, as he never lost a battle; therefore, I knew he would kill us all. I thank God for

Nabal's servant came to me with the news so we could intercept a catastrophe. Over the years, I've learned the warfare strategy of intercession and humbleness. It saved our lives and gave me more than I ever thought I would have.

1 Samuel 25

Then David moved down to the wilderness of Maon.[a] 2 There was a wealthy man from Maon who owned property near the town of Carmel. He had 3,000 sheep and 1,000 goats, and it was sheep-shearing time.3 This man's name was Nabal, and his wife, Abigail, was a sensible and beautiful woman. But Nabal, a descendant of Caleb, was crude and mean in all his dealings.

4 When David heard that Nabal was shearing his sheep, 5 he sent ten of his young men to Carmel with this message for Nabal: 6 "Peace and prosperity to you, your family, and everything you own! 7 I am told that it is sheep-shearing time. While your shepherds stayed among us near Carmel, we never harmed them, and nothing was ever stolen from them. 8 Ask your own men, and they will tell you this is true. So would you be kind to us, since we have come at a time of celebration? Please share any provisions you might have on hand with us and with your friend David." 9 David's young men gave this message to Nabal in David's name, and they waited for a reply.

40

10 "Who is this fellow David?" Nabal sneered to the young men. "Who does this son of Jesse think he is? There are lots of servants these days who run away from their masters. 11 Should I take my bread and my water and my meat that I've slaughtered for my shearers and give it to a band of outlaws who come from who knows where?"

12 So David's young men returned and told him what Nabal had said.13 "Get your swords!" was David's reply as he strapped on his own. Then 400 men started off with David, and 200 remained behind to guard their equipment.

14 Meanwhile, one of Nabal's servants went to Abigail and told her, "David sent messengers from the wilderness to greet our master, but he screamed insults at them. 15 These men have been very good to us, and we never suffered any harm from them. Nothing was stolen from us the whole time they were with us. 16 In fact, day and night they were like a wall of protection to us and the sheep. 17 You need to know this and figure out what to do, for there is going to be trouble for our master and his whole family. He's so ill-tempered that no one can even talk to him!"

18 Abigail wasted no time. She quickly gathered 200 loaves of bread, two wineskins full of wine, five sheep that had been slaughtered, nearly a bushel[b] of roasted grain, 100 clusters of raisins, and 200 fig cakes. She packed them on donkeys 19 and said to her servants,

"Go on ahead. I will follow you shortly." But she didn't tell her husband Nabal what she was doing.

20 As she was riding her donkey into a mountain ravine, she saw David and his men coming toward her. 21 David had just been saying, "A lot of good it did to help this fellow. We protected his flocks in the wilderness, and nothing he owned was lost or stolen. But he has repaid me evil for good. 22 May God strike me and kill me[c] if even one man of his household is still alive tomorrow morning!"

23 When Abigail saw David, she quickly got off her donkey and bowed low before him. 24 She fell at his feet and said, "I accept all blame in this matter, my lord. Please listen to what I have to say. 25 I know Nabal is a wicked and ill-tempered man; please don't pay any attention to him. He is a fool, just as his name suggests.[d] But I never even saw the young men you sent.

26 "Now, my lord, as surely as the Lord lives and you yourself live, since the Lord has kept you from murdering and taking vengeance into your own hands, let all your enemies and those who try to harm you be as cursed as Nabal is. 27 And here is a present that I, your servant, have brought to you and your young men. 28 Please forgive me if I have offended you in any way. The Lord will surely reward you with a lasting dynasty, for you are fighting the Lord's battles. And you have not done wrong throughout your entire life.

29 "Even when you are chased by those who seek to kill you, your life is safe in the care of the Lord your God, secure in his treasure pouch! But the lives of your enemies will disappear like stones shot from a sling!30 When the Lord has done all he promised and has made you leader of Israel, 31 don't let this be a blemish on your record. Then your conscience won't have to bear the staggering burden of needless bloodshed and vengeance. And when the Lord has done these great things for you, please remember me, your servant!"

32 David replied to Abigail, "Praise the Lord, the God of Israel, who has sent you to meet me today! 33 Thank God for your good sense! Bless you for keeping me from murder and from carrying out vengeance with my own hands. 34 For I swear by the Lord, the God of Israel, who has kept me from hurting you, that if you had not hurried out to meet me, not one of Nabal's men would still be alive tomorrow morning." 35 Then David accepted her present and told her, "Return home in peace. I have heard what you said. We will not kill your husband."

The more my husband's servant spoke, the more my heart dropped.

"He screamed insults at them."

"You need to know this and figure out what to do."

43

"For there is going to be trouble for our master and his whole family."

"He's so ill-tempered that no one can even talk to him!"

I am grateful for the relationships I had with my husband's servants. Had he not felt comfortable coming to me and took the matter into his own hands, it would have ended in tragedy. I cannot express the value in treating people with dignity and respect. Be sure that those God put in your path to serve you are more than just a servant. God has hand picked them for you and they are warriors just like you. The victory cannot be won apart from God and them. They are strategic in revealing the plans of the enemy to you and facts you need to know to win the war. Partner with them as they are pivotal to your warfare.

I had no time to contemplate should I speak to Nabal if this was true or not. *I wasted no time*….My sister, there will be times, if you haven't experienced it already, where you will not have time to justify warfare. You will hear news that will devastate you, but don't let it paralyze you. Allow this news to fuel your strategies on how to combat the enemy before it's too late. I wasted no time and quickly gathered provisions, packed them on donkeys and gave instructions to my servants to go on ahead of me, and I would follow shortly.

When I saw David, I quickly got off my donkey and bowed low before him. There's that word again - *quickly*. Hesitation is not needed in warfare. Some things you need to do quickly as it may be a matter of life and death. I didn't have time to stay at home and pray for a solution. I had to be ready and stay ready as the solution. Getting off my donkey, bowing low, and falling at David's feet are warfare strategies that immediately intercept the enemy. The enemy loves pride; therefore, when you humble yourself, it softens the defenses and can change the trajectory of an attack.

"I accept all blame in this matter, my lord." I couldn't believe the words when they came out of my mouth. Everyone, including me, knew it was because of Nabal we were in the middle of the territory leading to the battlefield; yet, as a wife, I took seriously my vow of the two shall become one. Let me talk to the wives for a minute.

Wives, I was living, having sex with, and surrounded by a wealthy husband who threw parties, was ill-tempered, mean, a drunk, and wicked in his dealings. Some days were unbearable. Others were merry. Did the good outweigh the bad? I cannot say. Did the wealth help? Only in instances were it could be a blessing to others. Did I communicate with my husband? Absolutely. I learned the value in the perfect timing. When I went to meet David, I didn't tell my husband (vs. 19) because I know the power of moving silently in intercession. But, after he sobered up from his party the next day, I told him what happened (vs.37). The news caused him to have a stroke, become paralyzed, and ten days later, the Lord struck him, and he died.

What does this part of my story say to you? I don't know who you are married to. He may have some of the qualities of Nabal, be worse, or not as bad. Regardless, learn this from me: your husband may be the cause of your warfare, but God can use you to combat it and release you from it. God has the final say!

Back to my story - the end of it. David received my apologies and accepted the gifts. When he heard Nabal was dead, he gave God praise for avenging the insults and for keeping him from doing what only God can do. *Sometimes our warfare is not just for us to win, but it can benefit the lives of those who comes against us.*

David's messengers came asking me to be his wife, and I bowed low to the ground again giving my acceptance and *quickly* getting ready, I took five of my servant girls, mounted my donkey, and went with them to be David's wife (vs. 42). I stayed humbled, and I moved quickly. I am a Woman Who Warred.

Declarations

- I engage warfare quickly as God leads me.

- People come to me because I have the solution to the problem.

- God has provisions and people in position to help me war.

- I don't allow the character of my spouse to deter me from my destiny.

- I communicate with my spouse on God's timing and in his way.

- I can take blame for my spouse's behavior as it honors God and nullifies the plans of the enemy.

- I trust that God will avenge me.

- I war through humbleness and have respect for authority.

- Catastrophes are ceased because of my intercession.

- God favors me with others because of my intercession.

Prayer

Father, despite all that I have been through, you've been there with me. Thank you for teaching me how to war via intercession and having people in place to carry out your strategies and plan. I know that I am not perfect, and sometimes my spouse's character makes it challenging for me to remain in this marriage. Teach me how to love him and remain faithful. Help me to remember to war with humbleness and respect. Let me know when I should speak to my spouse and when to remain silent. Help me to respond quickly knowing you will avenge me and the ultimate victory belongs to you, and you will get the glory. In Jesus name, Amen.

CHAPTER 6

DECEPTIVE WARFARE

Warrior: Victoria

War Zone: My Home

Enemy or Opposition: Anger, Insecurity, My Tongue

Strategies and Weapons: Prayerful silence, Mastering my Tongue, Open Heart

Scriptures: Psalm 139 23-24, Philippians 4:8, Matthew 18:19-20

I was enjoying life loving on my family. I was ready for the next thing God had for us. I thought we overcame a huge trial in our marriage and nothing can stop us now. Well, it was not long after that, something would put me to the test. Would I recognize my real enemy? Would I be able to use my weapons? Would I even know which weapons I have to use? The same spirit of anger and insecurity tried to raise its head back again in our marriage. I remember sitting and trying to figure out how the argument started; why was I so upset?

Sometimes I would trace it back to a small something and other times I never discovered what was the starting point. I knew something had to be different this time. I couldn't keep handling this the same way. I prayed, but I never really listened to what God was saying about me. I was always listening to hear what He would tell me about my husband.

It was during this time that God connected me to some powerful women of God. The group of women who birthed the Facebook Community, Women Who War. The women and I would meet and have prayer daily. We fasted and prayed and grew spiritually. God was dealing with each of us individually. Letting us know specifics of where we were lacking. For me, I needed to increase my prayer life so I could be a better wife and mother. I needed to become more intimate with God and allow Him to love me as my father so I could receive all the benefits of being his daughter.

Through this process of prayer and fasting and becoming more intimate with God, I recognized that I had a wall up around my heart. I had found the root. The starting point of so many arguments in my marriage. It was me, my wall! Me not allowing my husband to fully see or love me. I kept myself guarded against being hurt. I did not see this all those years before, but it was true. I was protecting myself from being hurt again. I was so devastated as a little girl when my dad died that I protected myself by not letting others in. I was not aware that this was happening but through this time of prayer and fasting God revealed it to me. I was the source. I had kept my Mark at a distance. I did not allow him to get as close as he wanted or even I wanted him to. I longed for the affection, but then I would stop it before it could even become a thought.

So, now I could see how arguments started because I would not allow him to take control and be our family's head. There were times I would snap at a simple question. I had to take inventory and see myself through his eyes. God showed me myself. I had to step back and take my place as the wife who fully supports her husband. When Mark made a decision, I supported him. Whether I agreed or not, thought it was a good idea or not, I had to learn how to allow him to operate in his role as head of our household. There were situations I knew I was right, and I would say nothing. I went along with Mark's decision. I was expecting to hear disappointing news but on the contrary. It was great news. Yes, he can make a decision without my help. I smile about this now, but oh when we were going through this struggle. I was not smiling.

This was a constant scene for us. With time and prayer, I learned to value and rely on Mark's decision-making skills. I also had to learn to close my mouth and allow God and Mark to handle things. When I did that, peace followed in our home. I have to share though, that there were times I felt we should do something and Mark disagreed, so we did not do it. Then, it would happen. Mark would come and say you were right. I should have listened to you. This conversation would have never occurred between us before if I had not learned how to close my mouth.

Taming my tongue was difficult. I thought I knew best. I grew up with a single mother who appeared to do it all. I really thought I knew best. But when God got through with me, I knew I knew nothing and was grateful for another chance to get it right.

God had given me divine downloads about my family during this time of prayer with my new spiritual sisters. God showed me so much and made it very clear I had to get myself in proper spiritual alignment to receive the bountiful blessings he has for my family. God would bless my household, but I had to conquer this first. I had to master my tongue and break down the walls that guarded my heart. How did that happen? I met a powerful group of women who were not afraid to war with me for my family. I am in right spiritual alignment reaping the benefits of an intimate relationship with God, my Father.

CHAPTER 7

IN LAW WARFARE

WARRIOR: Twinette

WAR ZONE: My home

ENEMY/OPPOSITION: Spirits who had access via my mother-in-law

STRATEGIES & WEAPONS: Prayer, a clean house sweep, and a conversation with my husband

---

Behold, I give unto you power to tread on serpents and scorpions, and over all the power of the enemy: and nothing shall by any means hurt you. <u>Luke 10:19</u> -

It began in 2014 when I made a conscious decision with my husband to bring my mother-in-law into our home so she would no longer have to be alone in the rural mountain area of Fredonia Kentucky. At that point and time, her own children had not come to her aid or recognized she could no longer survive on her own and maintain a normal household. So my husband packed up all her belongings and moved her to South Carolina.

That was the beginning of the biggest fight I have ever experienced... one where I almost lost myself, my spirit and my mind! But thank GOD, He never allowed me to lose my faith, and that was the catalyst that kept me covered and secured. He was my strength when I was weak and gave me the power to call on my warring angels when I could no longer fight!

My home is my sanctuary and few people, outside of my husband, children and immediate family have access to it. Even though I understood what evil spirits were, I never had to fight them in my home because they never had an opportunity to enter. But my mother-in-law, in a subtle and cunning way, brought in spirits that made my home their dwelling place. Demonic forces like wrath, rage fury spirit, manipulation, lying, and drunkenness.

For three years, my mother-in-law and the spirits she accepted and befriended turned my home upside down with me in it! The torment began with smoking and drinking, and I tried to give her something she enjoyed because she no longer had her own life and had to become a part of ours. WRONG. I quickly learned I gave all her demons authority. The act of an occasional drink took on the forms of alcoholic fits of rage, cursing, rude behavior, racist name-calling, and the physical destruction of my house and furniture. She

54

also manipulated my husband, into thinking she loved him more than me and persuaded him to think I was causing problems in his life which lead to massive heated arguments all the time. My husband separated himself from me, he did things to hurt my feelings, including verbal abuse, separating bills and household responsibilities, he even drank and formed alliance pity parties with his mother against me.

My mother-in-law also called her family members and friends, spread lies about my home and the dynamics of it and who I was. She would sneak around through my belongings and invite herself to our movie nights, dinners, and would stay in the room when a guest came to see us. One vivid memory that took things to a point of no return, was that she entered the closed door of our bedroom without knocking or announcing herself during our private time together. I withdrew so much that I would welcome going to a job I didn't like, just to come home and go straight to my bedroom and lock myself in it until the next morning. During the third year, she drank from sun up to sun down, did not bathe, and had dysentery accidents in her room and my main bathroom. It was so bad my home reeked of fecal matter, urine and old body odor. No matter how much I tried to clean or cover it up, the demons that had taken root and charge of my home were there to stay...... so they thought! One Saturday morning while my husband was working, I woke up at 5 am and determined enough was enough, too much was too much, and I needed GOD to help me!

I played warfare prayers from John Eckhardt & Dr. Cindy Trimm on my living room TV, turning the volume up to the highest level available. Then I screamed and prayed to the top of my lungs, calling on my warring angels to come and destroy everything that had attached itself to the walls, the furniture, clothing, electronics, and anything in my home that had a name all while opening my doors and windows. I did this from 5 am until 10 am and during this entire time my mother-in-law never came out of her room. Later on that evening, she immediately told my husband she was afraid (and I'm sure every demon in her was because they knew their time was up!)

The boldness in my spirit was still there, and I explained to my husband this could no longer continue. Without, an argument or any long discussion, he looked at me and said - I AGREE! And within a 2-week period, we packed her up and moved her into a nursing home 0were she is to this day.

I understood and respected the power of the Lord, and how he would always fight my battles no matter the size. God's word again came to pass and after only a year, her health failed:

Deut 28:22   [22] The LORD shall smite thee with a consumption, and with a fever, and with an inflammation, and with an extreme burning, and with the sword, and with blasting, and with mildew; and they shall pursue thee until thou perish.

So I leaned on GOD again this time to help me with complete forgiveness, and visited her regularly for hours at a time, giving her things she needed, things that made her happy, because the devil had left her in shambles. Alzheimer was setting in and she could no longer take care of herself, and she rarely had visits from her children (all of them lived in another state, but rarely found time to visit her) and her other family members were deceased. That's when it happened.

Psalm 110:1 "Sit at my right hand until I make your enemies a footstool for your feet.".

She asked for me, and when I visited she would light up and know who I was while she continued to forget others. She would even tell the nurses I was her daughter, and she loved me, GOD is so amazing! The breakthrough came, and I won the war!

CHAPTER 8

QUICKLY WAR

WARRIOR: ZIPPORAH

WAR ZONE: On the road to Egypt

OPPOSITION: The Lord Himself

STRATEGIES & WEAPONS: Quick response in obedience to God

Zipporah's Story

I and my six sisters experienced his kindness as he jumped up and rescued us from shepherds. Then he drew water for our flocks. Someone dressed him like an Egyptian, but his hospitality reminded me of a Hebrew. When my sisters and I returned to our father Reule, he asked: "Why are you back so soon today?" We told him how the Egyptian rescued us, drew water, and watered our flocks. It's peculiar that an Egyptian knew how to do those things because normally their slaves did it. My father urged us to go back to him and invite him to come and eat with us. That one day changed my life forever.

Exodus 2:15b - 22;

But Moses fled from Pharaoh and went to live in the land of Midian.

When Moses arrived in Midian, he sat down beside a well. **16** Now the priest of Midian had seven daughters who came as usual to draw water and fill the water troughs for their father's flocks. **17** But some other shepherds came and chased them away. So Moses jumped up and rescued the girls from the shepherds. Then he drew water for their flocks.

18 When the girls returned to Reuel, their father, he asked, "Why are you back so soon today?"

19 "An Egyptian rescued us from the shepherds," they answered. "And then he drew water for us and watered our flocks."

20 "Then where is he?" their father asked. "Why did you leave him there? Invite him to come and eat with us."

Moses accepted the invitation, and he settled there with him. In time, Reuel gave Moses his daughter Zipporah to be his wife.

22 Later she gave birth to a son, and Moses named him Gershom, for he explained, "I have been a foreigner in a foreign land."

24 On the way to Egypt, at a place where Moses and his family had stopped for the night, the Lord confronted him and was about to kill him. **25** But Moses' wife, Zipporah, took a flint knife and circumcised her son. She touched his feet with the foreskin and said, "Now you are a bridegroom of blood to me." **26** (When she said "a bridegroom of blood," she was referring to the circumcision.) After that, the Lord left him alone.

Zipporah's Story

Being married to Moses was interesting. I thought our lives would be normal as we raised our sons, and he tended the flock of my father as a great shepherd. All of that normalcy went away the day Moses lead the flock far into the wilderness to Sinai, the mountain of God. In his words, God spoke to him through a burning bush instructing him to lead His people Israel out of Egypt. When he returned home, he looked pretty shook up as he spoke to my father asking his blessing to return to Egypt. Moses packed our belongings, put us and our sons on a donkey and headed to the land of Egypt.

I didn't know what to think at this point. Moses was quiet on the ride and wouldn't put down his staff. I had never been away from my family and didn't know how I would be received in a foreign land. I am a Cushite woman and in Moses' culture, he should marry a Hebrew. His brother Aaron and sister Miriam criticized Moses because he married me, and the Lord heard them and dealt with them harshly (Numbers 12). Let me encourage you: if you experience in-law drama, trust me that God will not allow you to suffer through all of your marriage. Moses' love for me buffered me from most of it, but I saw the looks on their faces and how they avoided me as much as possible. Still, I didn't allow how they treated me to determine how I would treat them, and neither should you.

Not everyone will rejoice about who God has you to marry. God destined Moses and me to be together. He knew I would be the one who could handle being married to a leader, a prophet of this magnitude. God chose me to marry Moses because his past didn't taint what I thought of him nor was I impressed with him as an Egyptian. I fell in love with him when he was at his lowest, when he could have easily ignored us, yet in his darkest hour, he brought light to our situation. Because he protected us from the shepherds, I knew he would protect me in our marriage. That's the only Moses I knew and came to love.

On the way to Egypt, we stopped at a place for the night, and the Lord confronted Moses and was about to kill him! You could say I took matters into my own hands as I grabbed the flint knife, circumcised our son and presented the foreskin to Moses. Many speculate exactly what does that mean, but for our purposes, let's focus on the what instead of the why.

Have you ever faced a situation that was life or death for your spouse?

Can you recall a time in your marriage when you know your husband was out of the will of God and had to take quick action?

How did you war?

For me, I knew who the Lord was when He appeared because of my personal relationship with Him. I learned to be submissive and obey my husband and didn't question him in matters of what God told him to do. But in this moment, I didn't want God's wrath to be upon my husband because of his disobedience. What I did, how I warred by quickly obeying God, not only saved my husband's life, but it also placed him back in the will of God.

There may be times, my sister, when your warfare requires you to take action immediately, to do what you know to do, and inflict pain. If you have children like me, you never want to cause intentional pain on them; yet, you know to choose your husband first. That's not popular in many marriages. As a mother, it's ingrained in us to nurture and spend time with our children and many times our husbands take a back seat. Now, don't get me wrong, to everything there is a season. When my sons were infants and toddlers, I gave attention to them more than Moses. At the same time, Moses was my priority. After I warred, by quickly obeying God and inflicting pain for a purpose, the Lord left Moses alone, and he was back in His will.

There is so much more I could share with you about supporting your husband as he leads, how to deal with insults and complaints from those he led, and not being able to spend a lot of time with him. My husband saw but didn't get to cross over into, the promised land. Once again, his disobedience to God was costly, and this time I couldn't intervene to stop it. There were difficult times in our marriage, but the good outweighed the bad. Seeing him persevere in the face of Pharaoh time and time again, watching God use him when we faced the Red Sea, and all the miracles God used him to perform were amazing. I don't know what you're facing with your spouse in this season of your life, but this one thing I know, if God put you with your husband, you can face anything. Be in tune to know when you need to step in and partner with God to align back in His will. Obey God no matter what and be a woman who wars.

Declarations

- I obey God and do what needs to be done for my husband to be in the will of God.

- Although some may criticize my marriage, I let the Lord handle it as vengeance is His.

- I support my husband through the good and the bad.

- I willingly let go of what I think should be a normal marriage to embrace the destiny He has in store for my family.

- I honor the decisions my husband makes and allow him to be the leader God has chosen him to be.

Prayer

Father, show me how to support my husband in every season of our lives. Sometimes I desire a "normal" marriage, but if that is not the path you have for us, prepare him, me and our children for it. Thank you for showing me from the beginning the character of my spouse. Show me how to cultivate that in our children in a way that pleases You. I pray that my husband's relationship with you is so close he can have one-on-one conversations with you. Allow me to be okay with sharing him with others and protect my heart from hearing insults and complaints from those he leads. When he faces the enemy, pharaohs, show me how to support and pray for him. Help me to always walk in forgiveness and love knowing we don't wrestle against flesh and blood, but against principalities, against powers, against the rulers of darkness of this world, and against spiritual wickedness in high places. Help me to know the seasons and times when I should choose my husband before I choose my children. I cannot be a wife without you, Lord. I depend on you. In Jesus' name, Amen.

CHAPTER 9

MY OWN WORST ENEMY

WARRIOR: Sarah

WAR ZONE: Her home.

ENEMY/OPPOSITION: Hagar by way of Sarah/barrenness

STRATEGIES & WEAPONS: None.

Sarah's Story

I left with my husband not knowing exactly where we were going. He complimented me often by saying I was a very beautiful woman. When he told me to lie and say I was his sister, I did. Because I submitted to him and lied, he received many gifts from Pharaoh. When he and our nephew's men were disputing, I watched him give up the good land. When our nephew was in the middle of a war, my husband risked his life and the lives of his trained men to rescue him. Amid all of this, God promised us a child in our old age, but I was anxious and took matters into my hands. My story is to show you more so how NOT to war than HOW to war. I became my enemy. I am the woman who caused the war.

Genesis 16:1-6 NIV

Now Sarai, Abram's wife, had borne him no children. But she had an Egyptian slave named Hagar; 2 so she said to Abram, "The Lord has kept me from having children. Go, sleep with my slave; perhaps I can build a family through her."

Abram agreed to what Sarai said. 3 So after Abram had been living in Canaan ten years, Sarai his wife took her Egyptian slave Hagar and gave her to her husband to be his wife. 4 He slept with Hagar, and she conceived.

When she knew she was pregnant, she began to despise her mistress.5 Then Sarai said to Abram, "You are responsible for the wrong I am suffering. I put my slave in your arms, and now that she knows she is pregnant, she despises me. May the Lord judge between you and me."

6 "Your slave is in your hands," Abram said. "Do with her whatever you think best." Then Sarai mistreated Hagar; so she fled from her.

Genesis 21:1-11

Now the Lord was gracious to Sarah as he had said, and the Lord did for Sarah what he had promised. 2

Sarah became pregnant and bore a son to Abraham in his old age, at the very time God had promised him.

Sarah's Story

I did what I thought was the right thing to do. I had not been able to bear children for my husband, and I believed the Lord prevented me from having them. So yes, I had a conversation with Abraham and gave my Egyptian servant Hagar to him as a wife, and she became pregnant. We thought we would help God fulfill the promise he gave to Abraham, but it complicated the entire situation.

Have you ever "helped" God out? Have there been times when you took matters into your own hands because you thought "this has to be the way because I don't see another way this will work?" Speaking from experience of being a "fixer," let me caution those who have not did it: stay out of it. Just take God at his word and patiently wait on the promise. My life would have been totally different had I just waited on God's timing and His way. His thoughts are not our thoughts, and neither are His ways our ways (Isaiah 55:8-9). If nothing else, I knew how intimate of a relationship Abraham had with God and could have asked for clarity. If you have a husband who loves and communes with God like mine did, please don't intervene in the plans they discussed. Learn from me and trust the God in Him. Take it a step further and cultivate your love relationship with the Lord so that you know you hear from Him too and have confirmation.

Keep in mind, I'm not telling you to do as I did. Learn from me. Because I didn't wait on God, war broke out. Hagar begin to mistreat me with contempt, thinking she was beneath me because she was pregnant, and I went off. "This is all your fault!" I said to Abraham. "I put my servant into your arms, but now that she's pregnant she treats me with contempt. The Lord will show who's wrong - you or me!" Abraham gave me permission to deal with her as I saw fit. I treated Hagar so harshly that she finally ran away. Sigh...even having to tell you what I said makes me shutter.

I was to blame.

I became my own worst enemy.

The lies.

The deceit.

The manipulative behavior to help God out.

The mistreatment of a pregnant woman whom I had a relationship with prior.

69

The way I yelled at my husband, blaming him.

The relief I felt when she ran away.

I was wrong on all levels.

I created the war zone.

I wasn't a woman who warred. I was the woman who caused the war.

Thank God He didn't allow my manipulative behavior to stop the promise. That's good news for you as well. God is so loving and will still do what He said He would do despite us. God had every right to withdraw his promise after the way I intervened and mistreated Hagar; yet, in His sovereignty He changed my name from Sarai to Sarah and told Abraham, "I will bless her and give you a son from her! Yes, I will bless her richly, and she will become the mother of many nations. Kings of nations will be among her descendants." (Gen. 17:16)

It took 15 years for the promise to come to pass, and a year before I gave birth, I laughed in doubt. The Lord questioned my laughter and asked, "Is anything too hard for the Lord?" I stood on that Word, and I want you to do the same. No matter what you face, my sister. No matter how much you may have made a mess of your life and the lives of other. If God has made you a promise, and it seems impossible, always remember, nothing is too hard for the Lord.

A year later, I birthed my promise, Isaac. I wish I could tell you that all was well after Isaac was born, but it wasn't. Ishmael made fun of Isaac, and I demanded Abraham to get rid of Hagar and him. Abraham didn't want to, but God told him, "Do not be upset over the boy and your servant. Do whatever Sarah tells you, for Isaac is the son through whom your descendants will be counted." Although I reacted in anger, God used it to confirm to Abraham that it's part of His plan.

I hope my story will help you learn how to avoid creating a war in your home. Our husbands deal with so much outside of the home and need peace inside of it. Ask God to help you create a sanctuary in your home and show you how to help your spouse wait patiently for the promise from Him. Be the wife who wars and not the wife who creates the war.

Declarations

- I am a woman who wars and not a woman who creates a war.

- I believe the promise of God and will not manipulate it to come to pass.

- I patiently wait on the promise knowing it will come to fruition in God's timing and way.

- I won't put my husband in a position that compromises our marriage bed.

- I consult with my husband for confirmation of the promise.

- I cultivate my love relationship with the Lord.

- I believe that nothing is too hard for the Lord.

- I believe God will bless me despite me.

Prayer

Father help me to believe what you say about me and not get in the way of your plans. Forgive me for the times when I took things in my own hands and made a mess of it. Thank you for cleaning it up and putting my husband and I back on the path you have for us. You have my permission to change me and my name to line up with the destiny you have for my life. Help me support my husband and not be manipulative. As the timing for the promise lingers, help me to be patient and not rush it. Let me always remember that even though it seems impossible and goes outside the normal timing of things, nothing is too hard for you. In Jesus name, Amen.

CONCLUSION

Adrienne

Jael

Hannah

Deronda

Abigail

Victoria

Twinette

Zipporah

Sarah

(Insert your name)

We are Women Who War. As you were reading, which warrior did you identify most with? Whose story grabbed you and made you think, "She is talking to me!" Whoever it is, I encourage you to go back to that story, read it again, and ask yourself, "What was going on within me as I read this story?" Self-reflection is powerful as you sit with your feelings and journal. Yes, I want you to journal, what was happening to you as you read. Did you get angry? Were you sad? Did tears fall? Take some time to engross yourself in that place for healing.

Next, I want you to look at the strategies and choose at least one you want to implement today. If you need more insight as to how to carry out the strategy, ask the Holy Spirit to teach you. He may lead you to a book, a podcast, a class, or a person. Be open to however He wants to instruct you.

What will you do, starting today, to become a wife who wars for her marriage instead of a woman who fights? If you don't know where to start, let's start with prayer.

Father, I surrender to you. I let go of the fighter within and release the warrior to arise. I acknowledge I cannot be a wife apart from you. Help me to always remember who the real enemy is and that he is a defeated foe because of what Jesus did on the cross. Teach me how to war. Teach me the strategies I need most in my marriage. Help me not to give up too soon and throw in the towel. I want to be a wife who wars and wins! In Jesus' name, Amen.

About the Author

Adrienne Young is the Chief Visionary Warrior and Founder of Remnant Warriors Global, Inc., a nonprofit organization whose mission is for women and girls worldwide to know how powerful they are in God and to walk in their Kingdom authority. She gets to touch the lives of over 6,500 women from 10 countries, on a weekly basis via their Women Who War Facebook community. These women come together to fellowship in regional prayer gatherings, weekly Bible studies, and once a year for the Warriors United Conference.

She is also the President of Adrienne Young Ministries, LLC where she partners with God to teach women, they can have it when He is their all. In her business, she mentors women, consults with Fortune 500 companies, host workshops, and pens books to help people in their journey to turn their passions into purpose. Her first book, *Don't Go Thrifting Without Me*, was the number one Amazon bestseller in Fashion and Art.

Whether she is leading Bible studies, preaching the Word of God, writing blogs or books, or presenting practical ways to grow businesses and ministries, any encounter with Adrienne will push you into greatness to live your best life unto the Lord. Adrienne is married to Eddie, and they live in Fort Mill, SC with their two sons.

53031161R00055

Made in the USA
Columbia, SC
13 March 2019